Flowering Yourself

Courtney N. Brookins

Flowering Yourself
Courtney N. Brookins
Copyright © 2017 by Courtney N. Brookins

Printed in the United States of America.

First Printing, 2017

Layout and Design by Jeff M. Miller | *FiveJsDesign.com*

Image credits:
Vecteezy.com: frankmib6 | adobewankenobi | zhaolifang | hollmolly | zurzovan | matrixdesigner | commercialart
Freepik.com: Freepik | mariia_fr | garrykillian | irikul | Planella | Daria

Floral Content

Dedications

Dear girls,

I once felt I had to master everything before your existence … and to perfect the very things that needed correcting. Improve the very things that needed altering. But I now know one of the best ways I can live as an example for you is letting go of the need to be perfect. I am not perfect. Nor will I ever be. In fact, accepting my own flaws will help you understand how to accept yours and let go of the notion to the falsity of being perfect. Preceding you in accepting my own humanity allows you to accept yours. Dear children, you are flawed. But your flaws are beautiful. They are a part of you. Accept them. Acknowledge them. Honor them and work through them. Perfection is not real. But you are. All parts of you. Even the ones that you try to hide in the shadows of your own insecurities. But don't hide from yourself. Shine light into those areas. Examine them. Dig deeper. Find the truth in their existence. They're there to teach you. To help you meet new pieces within you. They're there waiting on you. As soon as you take the first step, you'll find the next thing that needs your attention. But if you look down, you'll see the very things you've overcome. If you look to the side, you'll see what was not allowed to step into your path. If you look in front of you, you'll see the very thing that is calling you. It's your destiny. It's your purpose. It wants you. It needs you. All of you. Every. Single. Piece.

Iyanna and Camara Lewis, you are my "sunshines" and you light up my world. Thank you for living authentically, joyously and fearlessly. I am your mother, but through you I learn so much. I am thankful to have been your vessel into the world and more so I am thankful that both of your spirits continually connect me to the decider of all of creation.

I love you dearly,

Mommy

Acknowledgments

I come as one, but I stand as ten thousand.
~Maya Angelou

Thanks to my mother, Melonese,
for always loving and supporting me.

My grandmother, Irma and the late Mary for being
exemplary examples of women. And every other woman who
has helped me along my journey of womanhood, mothering
and the voyage of self-love.

Introduction

Flowering Yourself is a poetic, self- love letter with the intentions of liberation through light, love and honesty. This poetic sharing is a warm dialogue about evolution, culture, femininity, ancestry, healing, and self-love.

I pray that it encourages you to love and liberate your inner being.

Brown is my Favorite Color

A Letter to my Daughters

i look at your big glorious eyes

in them i see hope

one set brown and round

the other the shape of almonds

chocolate delight

warm as the sun on the beach in the late afternoon

like kisses from the sun on your skin

as decadent as dark chocolate

oozing with warmth and sweetness

your eyes are as deep as the roots on a tree

full like coconuts and kiwis

fruitfull like soil that allows plants to grow

and bear fruit

musical,

like

guitars and cellos

brown like the wood in which they were created

golden like the saxophone, and trumpet

originals

like the origins of time from the women of the Nile,

Caribbean and Latin America

Strong and hopeful like Rosa, Harriet, Gwendolyn, Angela, and Maya

you have in you a *magic*

and it twinkles like fairy dust

my brown-eyed babies

use these eyes to see the good in people

use them to guide the touch of your brown hands

let them direct you and walk upright

with your strong brown back

make long strides with your determined legs

connect with your heart that beats under your brown chest

hold your brown head up high

proudly

and love your brown crown

which covers your shining glory

reflect the God that is in you both

connect with humanity

spread tolerance, peace and kindness

you are brown-eyed goddesses

jewels

unburied treasures

unbury your treasure

treasures don't stay buried

brown eyes

dream big

dream bold

gleam

glisten and hold

that glorious brown glow

Connecting to self

Sometimes
When I feel out of sync
I lie alone
With just me
And focus on the beat of my chest
Depths of my breaths
The peace of my mind
And I am calm
For I am at one with me

Inside me

Inside me
There's an inner voice
One that whispers
When I am on course
And yells
When I am not
It cautions me to follow my
ambitions
To pursue my dreams
To focus on my purpose

Inside me
There's an inner voice
Reminding me of my strength
Encouraging me to go higher
Asking me to believe in myself
Achieve greatness
Answer my calling

Inside me there's an inner voice
That recognizes my own beauty
Appreciates my individuality
Soothes my own soul
Produces tranquility and peacefully
accepts self

Inside me there's an inner voice
I must listen to it
I must believe God will guide
me down a path of bliss

Inside me there's an inner
voice
She's connected to me
She follows the guidance and
meditation of the most high
She's in sync with the highest
vibrations
She's familiar with God's voice
God calls
She listens
Inside me there's an inner voice

Sing Girl: The Uprising

An Unsung song
A story untold
Chordless melodies
Verse-less lines
Bridged by a
Repetitious chorus
Without a mere hum
How can she not sing her own song?
Suppressing the state of her own feelings
How can she lull the desires of her own heartbeat?
Pit pat
Pit pat
There are things she needs to say
But, she's afraid the vibrations of her own words
Will cause walls around her to come crashing down
Tumbling
Restructuring the reality
Of the world she knew
So she keeps herself silent

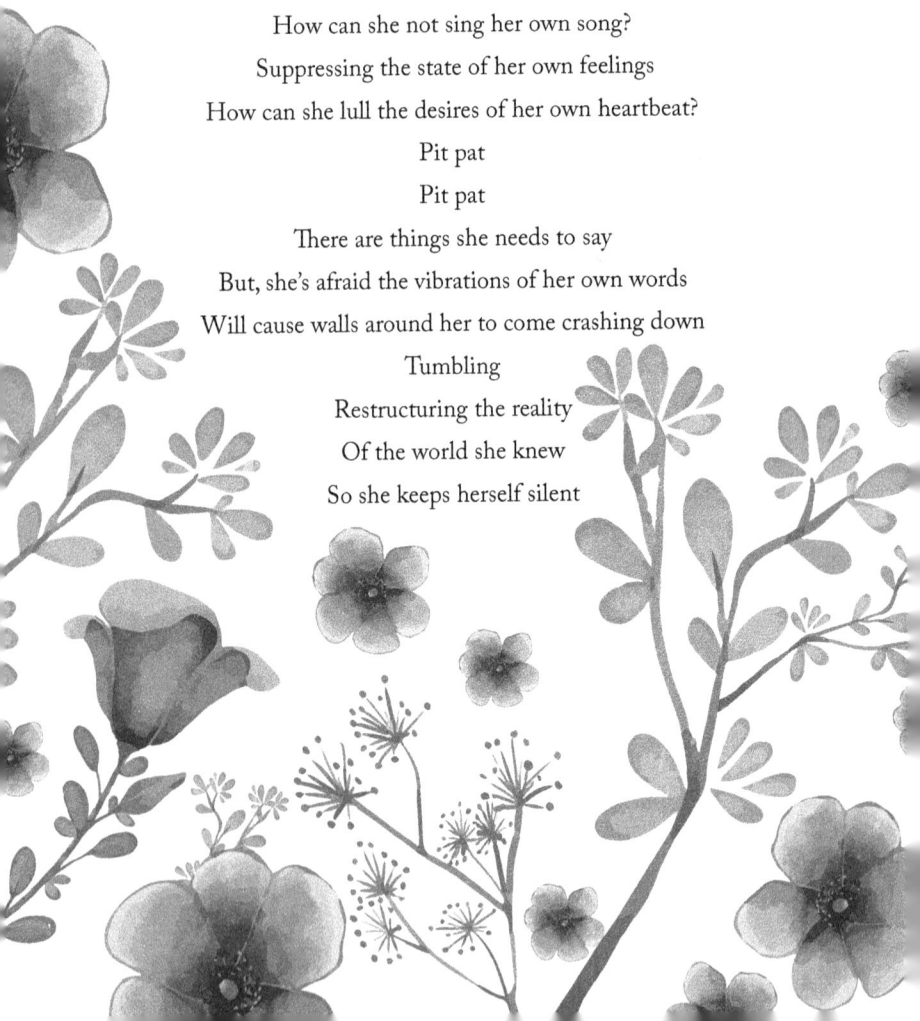

Reminding herself of a socialized ideology of femininity
Careful not to disturb the backbone of a man
Searching for his own identity.
She remains quiet
Silencing herself so her words don't offend him
Remaining silent as she strokes his ego
Strumming her own submission
Where is HER voice?
Why can't she talk?
She's choking on rhetorical female expectations
Coughing through the juxtaposed
Positioning of her internal cries
Internally shouting
She needs to speak.
But she remains silent
Auctioning off her submission in exchange for partnership
Petitioning a fictitious mirage of her self-concept
A misleading misconception of her self-image
She's not quiet

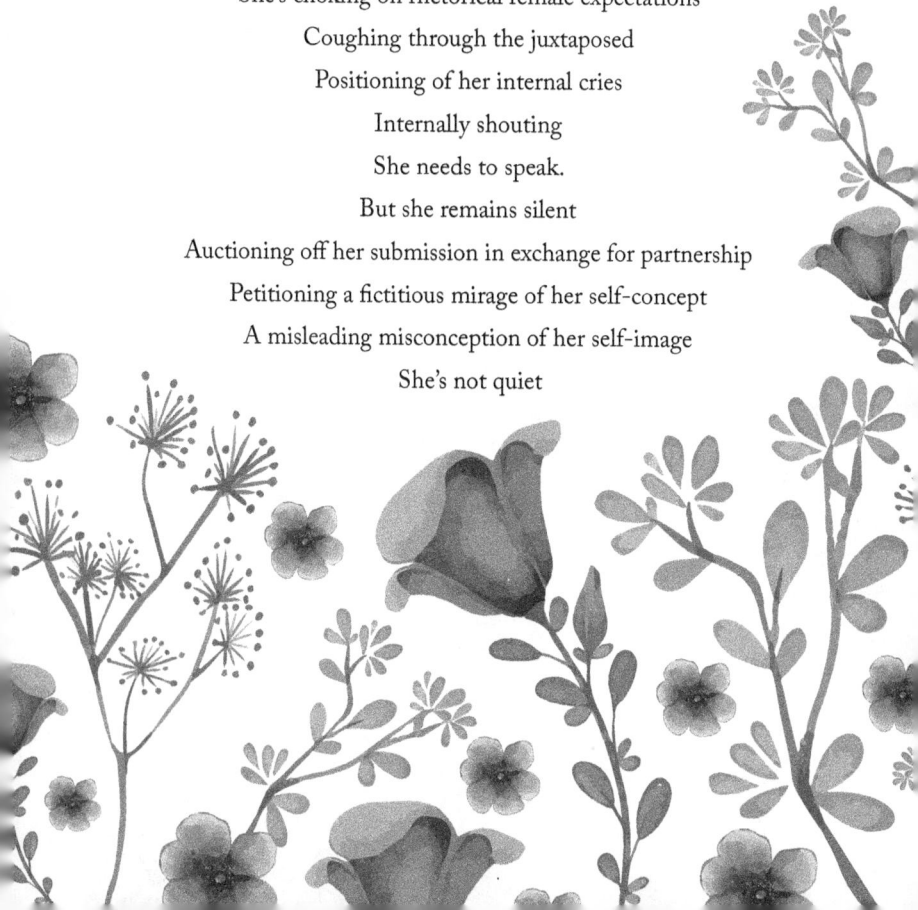

She has so much to say!

As her confidence blossoms

She's familiarized with the vibrations of her own tongue to her teeth

She's awakened to the voice inside of her

A voice that says

She is strong

A voice that says

She is beautiful

A voice that says

Her words liberate

Her beauty does not reside in the patriarchal concept of womanhood

She needs to define her Queendom

Serve in partnership next to a man who values her frequency

Her vibrations

Her voice

She is ready to speak

Tell her truth

Spread wisdom

With

Hymns from her ancestors

Mantras for daughters

Resounding her own story

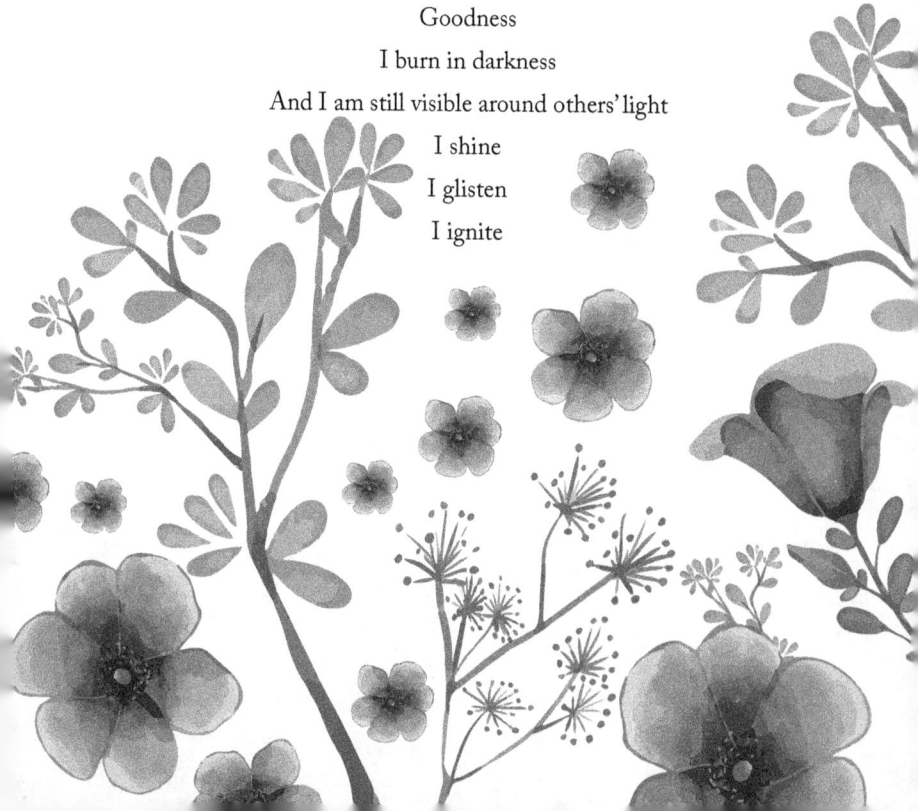

I am

I am a ball of fire

A light

That burns from within

That warms

I attract

Abundance

I attract

Peace

I attract

Goodness

I burn in darkness

And I am still visible around others' light

I shine

I glisten

I ignite

Balance

I once experienced a new light

His truths were old

And grounded in accuracy and wisdom

He taught me to experience the importance of balance

And acceptance

How to vacate my need for extremism

To find solace where I stand

To plant myself and to be rooted in the moment

For it is all we really have

So we must capitalize on it

This new light contrasted my attempts at midday rains

See, although I bought peace, growth and harvest

Finding the sun again was a reminder of his mission

Which was to teach balance

Through the weathered storms

Wind, fire and ice

Like changing seasons

I am reminded that it all traces back

Through death, we experience life

And through the darkness we find the appreciation of light

In this season of bloom I will not take my eyes off of the light

For it reminds me of his purpose

And guides me to mine

Balance I seek you

I need you

And I surrender to your gentle force

A New Light

Within me I see a new light
A different beauty that was not previously there
I feel myself
Growing, changing, wandering and being called
To new places and higher levels
Elevating
Furthering myself within myself
And seeking a new level of peace and understanding
Becoming tranquil
Becoming more at one with myself
A renewed outlook
One that acknowledges not only the God within the universe
But the God within me
Because if I am in God's image
And I follow light
Surely, I must shine too
I am blooming
I am glowing
A new seed has been planted
Indeed, I intend on nurturing it
Furthering my purpose and extending the glow from within me onto others

Within me I see a new light
I am practicing patience
And listening to the voice within my soul
Connecting to my higher source
Relying on it for my guidance
A new journey is beginning
I'm joyful for it
The seeds of my harvest have been planted

Within me I see a new light
One that is inspired
And inspiring
Emerging with grace
Praying for mercy
Healing old wounds by acknowledging them
Instead of hiding them
I am seeking honesty, truth, joy and hope
I am sewing those things into the world too
For you reap the seeds you sow
And you attract what you are
Within me I see a new light
One that is ready to love
Wholly and Completely
As intended by God
To be responsible
To keep God at the center of my heart
God is love
I must put all of my love, hope and trust within that
So I can have it for myself and feed it to someone else
God is my center and my core
And calling me to be great
Greatness is within me
I am encouraged

Within me I see a new light.
And it's warm.

Connectivity

I lie awake and I dream

I dream and I connect to the energy that empowers me and pushes me to

my highest self

I imagine

I see myself tapping into love

At its greatest level

connecting my soul

Unifying it with another's whose frequency matches mine

One that calms my fears

Inspires my delights

Supports my desires

I climax into a place of eroticism

Blissfully

Capturing the power of love

It propels me

It magnifies my touch

I am a queen

Created to touch generations

To connect people and things to something beyond their imagination

In me

I have the strength and energy to birth love

To challenge complacency

Mediocrity has no place here

As it never lived with my ancestors

I was born to make a change

To ignite light

To uplift those whose light crosses my path

I will continue to tap into everything created for me

Peace, warmth and love are vibrations that bounce off of me

Springing into the universe

As I connect more to myself

I absorb more of why I was created

That makes me powerful

Yet I humbly submit to the power that is greater than me

For my creator

Calls for me to be a light

And to submit to the greatest one

Through humility, honesty and love

To operate in dimensions of transparency

Using my heart and hand to be transformative

Freeing myself of the radicals which are useless energy i possess

I am in tune

I am love

I am peace

I am light

I am present

I am connected

I am that I am

For it is already in me

Dreaming

Inside us all
Lives a dream
A magical place full of passion and virtue
It is awaiting to be discovered
Give birth to what you already possess
For you've had it all along
The task was to merely discover it

Visualization

I dream
I dream of rooms filled with the floral scents of fresh flowers
And sheets with the soft scent of lavender
The warmth of light that fills a room
The vibration of love that sits there
cohesively
I dream of a man that grabs me
and pulls me into his masculinity
with a passionate kiss
I taste his being and feel his strength
I dream of orange and yellow scents
fresh oranges and lemons
which create an air of positivity
and newness
I dream of awakening

Tapping into the next level of self

Electrifying the gifts within me

The words potential, purpose and mission

Bounce in the room as if they are visually inscribed

I dream of a love

Which greets it all

That's so warm

I feel its glow

That's so helpful

I feel its touch

That's so supportive

It shadows me

I dream of me

experiencing it all

I am

happy

Love and Purpose

Explosion

Like some cosmic combustion

Here you come

Traveling through your mother's womb

Flowing through the path

That is only the beginning of the path you were created to travel

Your existence

Both ignited by energy, and love

Has brought you forth purposefully, intentionally and for reason

You were created with love

John 3:16

"God so loved the world that he gave his only son"

But he also gave sons and daughters

With different names

With significant purposes

You my child were not an accident

You are God-sent

God sent you

For a specific mission

The mission though sometimes seeming impossible

It is always calling you

Always seeking your face

Sometimes whispering to you like

The voice from within

OR touching you like the feeling of emotions that make you want to cry,

shout or seek action

Purpose is passion-filled

And it's also God-directed

It directs our path

And orders our steps in His name

So as you shout

"Oh, God, I want you to help me"

Know that help is on the way

As you lie there at his feet

Like Matthew 15:30

Know that Romans 8:28

Is still true

So thank God for every opened door and every closed one too

Because they've all guided you

Like GPS

God's programming system

Pointing you onward

Towards fulfillment

Of the very mission you were sent here to take on

That purpose

Though for some may be singular

For others have a coauthor

A mission mate

A person that compliments you

Like cornbread to greens

Like peanut butter to jelly

Like caramel to chocolate

You see I like food, don't you?

And like Boaz to Ruth

Purpose-mates

Two people coming together in ministry and servitude

Created for each other

But not coming together before they first did the work for their own

completion

They looked inward before onward

Examining the very needs of their souls

Listening to that guiding voice

Appraising their own hearts

Perpetuating self-dignity

Appreciating solitude

Conserving loyalty

Sauntering honorably

and obediently submitting to God's will

Self-mastery as its finest

Their work

Their story

A devotional

Just as much to their own journey as that of each other

Their story

Though not like

Romeo and Juliet

Alike having the resistance of coming from opposite sides of the tracks

Steered through the terrains of their own home front

Letting God be the captain

that guided them through the waters

Leading them to each other

Unifying them

Focalizing their destiny

Their relationship

an example of biblical romanticism

And the second-best love story

The greatest being God's love for us.

This story

an allegorical reminder

That God still loves you enough to make someone uniquely yours

to love you past your faults

To accept your journey

To walk with you

And to exemplify God's love for the world here on Earth

Through love.

Through relationship.

Through purpose.

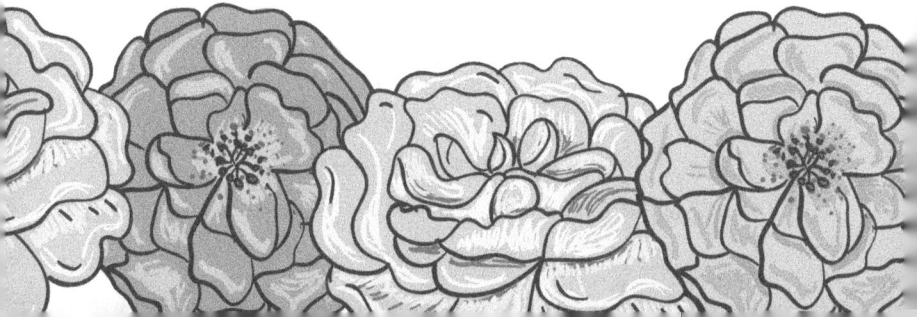

Seasons

Seasons

Bloom into your season

Blossom like a flower from its roots

Expanding past the dirt and soil

Pulling the soil's nutrients upward to feed and fuel your growth

Using the darkness

Beneath the soil

To strengthen your stems and stretch your petals upward toward the sun

Seasons

Germinate

Glow into existence

Develop despite dormancy

Using the droplets of rain

To water the moments of dryness

Using the coldness of winter

Season after season

Flourishing new color, new beauty, new fragrances

Blooming into a new creation

Becoming a new thing

In a grounded position

Seasons use the vitality of the sun

Your greatest resource comes from something way above you

Light rays highlight your journey

Warming your growth

Pulling you taller than yourself

Expanding you into what you were always created to be

Seasons

I once heard that

"No seed ever sees the flower. "

Yet I recognize that it grows anyway

Reaching its fullest level of bloom

Maturity

Spreading beyond its own florets

Pollinating others

Scattering to other locations

Leaving pieces of it in new areas

Helping others in their seasons of bloom

Creating a hue-ful ending out of a colorless beginning

Budding into Womanhood:
Lessons from a Flower

Baby:

Baby girl you are a seed that was planted
Intentionality all around your mother's womb
Sprinting to the finish line from the beginning
Beating out all of the other letters
Yes, X marks the spot
But hopefully your value will not be unknown or unnamed to you as you
matriculate into your next chapter.

Girl:

Hey, little girl.
I see your stem sprouting up
and your arms stretching wide
You're much bigger than seed you originated from
But don't lose sight of the origin of your seed
Originality is your framework
I hear the click-clack of your beads and barrettes
I love the chuckling sound of joy
It's innocent
That joy that you're so masterfully acquainted with comes from a space
from within so don't allow it to diminish when your eyes meet the unruly
and stereotypical expectation of an outside world.
Making you believe you need a prince for your own validation

Don't let Ariel and Cinderella
Be your only definition of princess because just because Disney "shows
you" white depictions of royalty Nefertiti and Cleopatra were on the scene
before animation … hey, girl

Teenager:
Oh, my, check you out.
Aren't you blooming?
You truly are a sight to see
You're blooming
Your buds have begun to open
Just make sure you know
You find the beauty in your own florets
Humans will try to class you by kingdom
But the kingdom which classified you already determined you were
Wonderfully and uniquely made
So when they tell you you're not shaded the right hue
Remember that your pigmentation
Was chosen from the moment that your seed was planted
That it will still attract bees
But be careful because your pollen is not meant for everyone to sample

Young woman:
Your flower is fully here
You have blossomed from the seed
Stretched your stem
Budded and fully bloomed
You have your petals
Just make sure you stay rooted
Look to the sun as your source of direction and energy
Rain will fall but learn to use it to aid your growth
Seasons will change but know that you are not an annual planting
The only things that die out after their planting
Are plants that were not meant to live in your quarters.
So if you find Impatiens, Marigolds and Zinnias
Scattering away from your garden
Recognize that is does not lessen the value of your flower
It just merely is a reminder that season has ended

Woman:
Woman
Seasons have come and gone
And you're still blooming
Weathering it all
I'm sure your roots have grown so wide and your stamen so full of pollen
That you aid the sustainability of the entire garden
Don't let your supporting the garden
Make you lose sight of your the beauty of your petals or the strength of

your stem
Do not grow weary in this space or lost in your aiding of other plants
And while you're spreading your pollen
Remember to keep a little of it for yourself
It's your magic and it's golden

Seasoned woman:
Hey, golden girl
Look at you glowing in your own self-worth
Look at you sharing your pollen as you please
Check you out, absorbing all that life has to offer
And colorfully reflecting
Light
You have learned to bloom where you are planted
Spreading your seeds
Producing your own fruit
Photosynthesizing
Synthesis of your production
You have mastered yourself
Weeding out the expectations of others
Recognizing your own cycles
Giving plentifully
And keeping enough for yourself
You share your beauty with the world
But you admire your own too.
That stem is strong
It remembers not only the journey from when it was first planted
It remembers the planter
And that is why you are so well-grounded.

Illumination

I want to illuminate myself
Fill myself up with joy, love and happiness
I want to create my own world
Full of peace and fullness
Finding comfort in my own energy
And expanding it to the layers within me
Leveling myself
And pushing it out into the world

Final Sharing

The great thing about life is that it is a journey not a destination. As you begin to explore yourself and examine the different pieces of you, you'll continuously make new discoveries. In writing this book, I unfolded new ways to love myself and recognized new pieces that had not been discovered. As a result, I am allowing myself to continue to bloom, grow, and spread my petals toward the sun.

Meet the Author

Courtney Brookins is a poet and creative living in Chicago, Illinois with her two daughters. She began writing in childhood and used her writings to explore her journey toward self-discovery and healing. Years later, her writings are fueled by her passion for community building, women's empowerment, self-care and self- love. She uses her poetry as a reflective platform to create warm and safe spaces through her literary sharings.

The following pages are for your exploration.

Open your petals.

Begin to flower yourself.

Floral Thoughts

_____

_____

_____

_____

_____

_____

_____

_____

_____

_____

_____

_____

_____

_____

_____

_____

_____

_____

Floral Thoughts

Floral Thoughts

Floral Thoughts

_____

_____

_____

_____

_____

_____

_____

_____

_____

_____

_____

_____

_____

_____

_____

_____

_____

Floral Thoughts

Floral Thoughts

_____

_____

_____

_____

_____

_____

_____

_____

_____

_____

_____

_____

_____

_____

_____

_____

_____

_____

Floral Thoughts

_____

_____

_____

_____

_____

_____

_____

_____

_____

_____

_____

_____

_____

_____

_____

_____

_____

_____

Floral Thoughts

_____

_____

_____

_____

_____

_____

_____

_____

_____

_____

_____

_____

_____

_____

_____

_____

_____